# SNOW GOLF

*Humorous Short Stories About*
*GOLF*

JOHN SOWER

Snow Golf

Copyright © 2024 by John Sower

All Rights Reserved

No part of this publication may be reproduced, distributed, or transmitted in any form or by any means, including photocopying, recording, or other electronic or mechanical methods, without the prior written permission of the publisher, except in the case of brief quotations embodied in critical reviews and certain other non-commercial uses permitted by copyright law.

This book is dedicated to my wife, sons, grandson, brothers, and friends with whom I have shared fun, friendship, success, failure, drama, and humor – while playing golf.

## Table of Contents

Snow Golf.................................................................. 1

The Terror Of The First Tee ...................................... 8

Blonds on the Golf Course........................................17

The Million-To-One Man .........................................23

Ice Golf 33

Snookered Again.......................................................39

My Almost "Perfect Game".......................................46

My Favorite Place In The World –
The Practice Range ..................................................55

Dad's Last Win..........................................................62

Our First Round At The Quarry ...............................70

Best 80th Birthday Present Ever ..............................78

# Snow Golf

It was cold as we drove north on the New Jersey Turnpike on a Saturday evening in late October – and the wind was blowing. The weather forecast predicted a high of 46 degrees and cloudy. I try not to play when it is below 45 degrees – with no wind – so I assumed my golf match on Sunday would be canceled.

I had been invited to play at the Fairfield Country Club in Southport, Connecticut, as a birthday present (my 58th) from my friend Jay. It is a challenging private course, and I have played there with him before. It is on the east side of an inlet along the Connecticut Sound – and it is exposed to the prevailing winds from the West.

Jay is a serious competitive golfer who plays in club tournaments. He shoots in the high 80s, and I am lucky to break 100. He has told me that he likes the competition as much as the golf itself, and he likes seeing his opponent handing him a few dollars after his matches. He is a classy guy and a great host. His rounds with me are social golf – not serious competition.

On Sunday morning, it was clear and beautiful – so I did not have a good excuse. I did not want to whimper to Jay that it was too cold. I had already called him once to say I had a foot problem and needed a cart. Jay prefers to walk. Truthfully, although I love to play, I would not have been heartbroken if Jay had canceled.

Thinking the weather would get warmer, we leisurely ate breakfast and drove out of Manhattan. Jay had not set a tee time. I later learned that he had hoped we would arrive earlier because a bad weather front was coming down from the North.

It had gotten colder when we arrived at the Club around noon. I ditched my trusty visor in favor of a warm rain hat and wore a wool sweater under my jacket instead of my favorite cotton vest. No balls were available at the tee area at the practice range – so we had to wander onto the range, practicing our chipping and gathering balls for our few practice shots from the tee area. I felt bulky and was not swinging comfortably.

The wind was steady – maybe ten mph out of the North – with enough of a nip that we kept our ungloved right hands in our pockets. Jay kept saying that he liked the cold weather and found it invigorating. He is a tough New Englander. I just thought it was cold. Years before, I had left the cold Midwest to live in Washington, DC, to avoid this weather.

The first hole was a disaster. I had only brought three new balls, and my first swing sliced one of them into the backyard of one of the big houses on the right side of the fairway. Jay had given me a first-hole mulligan to offset his home course advantage, plus one mulligan each for the back and front nine. I have a 21 handicap, and Jay has a 16, so he gave me strokes on five holes. We were playing match play – scoring by the holes – not total strokes.

My second drive was a pop-up, which did not even reach the fairway. Jay hit his usual 200+ yard drive to the center of the fairway – and we were off. I got an eight on the first hole, but Jay gave me a six to look better next to his par 5, and we moved on.

The next two holes are a blur – I felt the first snowflakes while teeing off on the $2^{nd}$. I tried to ignore them. I think I tied Jay on one of these holes and lost the other one – I was in a trance because of the numbing cold.

The fourth hole was another disaster. It is a short 135-yard hole across a pond. I remembered that I had splashed it the last time I played. The wind was stronger, and it was now behind us. I splashed my $2^{nd}$ new ball on my first swing – which used up my front nine mulligan. I then splashed my water ball before over-shooting the hole with my third attempt – because the wind had increased to a two-club velocity.

I felt a sense of pending doom: I was already three holes behind, the wind was picking up, the sky was getting darker, and it was snowing steadily. I figured that

Jay would soon get bored of trouncing me and that we would quit after a few more holes.

The fifth hole is about 300 yards – as the crow flies – or as Tiger drives, but it is a 400-yard sharp dog-left right for the rest of us - with a scary second shot over the water to a small green which is "well protected" as they say by sand traps. My drive sliced again, and I had to take a penalty and a drop. My second shot, but third stroke, was pretty good and ended up about a yard over the green. I then dribbled my fourth stroke to end up a yard on the green. Jay had gotten on or near the edge of the green in two, but his next shot was short, leaving him a 12–15-footer. I sank my fifth shot – a miraculous, beautiful arching 25 ft putt that was pure luck, and I tied Jay with a 5 – except that I got a stroke because of my handicap and won the hole.

The sixth hole is a long dog leg to the right, and the drive needs 175 yards to clear the water. I hit my second miracle shot. I skipped my drive off the water – like a kid with a skipping stone – and it rolled into the center of the fairway – like the golf gods reached down through the snow to help me. I then laid up, hit decent $3^{rd}$ and chip shots – and won that hole because I got another stroke. I think we tied on the $7^{th}$, but I won the $8^{th}$ – it is a long par 5 along the beach, and I got a third stroke. I think, at this point, we were tied.

The tee-off for the ninth hole was awesome. It is about 160 yards headed north – a little uphill. I had hit a five iron to within five feet, my best shot of the day the last time I played. By now, the snow was coming down hard and horizontally – right into our faces – just like driving a car into a blizzard. I thought about using a three-wood but chickened out and hit a four-iron – which was a good shot but landed 30 yards short. It was at least a two-club wind and probably a three-club wind if you include the impact of the snow slowing the ball - a new experience for me.

We headed toward the clubhouse tied. Jay asked if I wanted a bowl of hot soup for lunch, but I declined because I was starting to feel it – entering a ZONE - and I did not want to break it by eating, relaxing, and getting warm. Jay, always the courteous host, politely consented to skip lunch.

The following 4-5 holes were wonderful. The snow was coming down hard – and it was coming at us horizontally because of the wind. I did not hit any more miracle shots, but I stayed in the zone, stayed confident, kept my eyes on the ball at impact, and mainly hit decent shots with no stupid errors. I learned that the snow does slow the ball in flight, and most of my shots were shorter than usual.

We saw several other golfers on the course – who were very bundled up but seemed happy. At one point, Jay and another guy shouted at each other simultaneously, "Are you crazy?"

By now, snow had accumulated on the greens - like dew early in the morning. We could see the trails of our putts through the snow. Jay had a normal reaction to the weather – and did not play his best golf. For some reason, the adverse conditions helped me concentrate – and I corrected my primary fallacy of not keeping my head down – and I hit many good shots. I did not lose any more balls nor even use my back nine mulligan. When in a zone, one expects to hit and does hit good shots.

We only talked about golf - the beauty of the game - total concentration. The fairways, club selection, wind directions, putting strategies, distances, scores, etc. No time for wives, children, business, friends, and politics – life's distractions from the game.

Somewhere in the snow, I moved ahead by two strokes – by taking advantage of the holes where I had strokes due to my higher handicap - then I picked up another one. I was up three holes! The cold dulled Jay's competitive instincts, and he slowly realized he had a problem. As soon as I had gotten ahead, I facetiously told Jay I was cold and wanted to quit and go home – but he adamantly responded, "No way." I think we tied 15th – which heightened the suspense - and Jay started getting more anxious.

The 16th is a 400-yard hole, with a fairway bunker on the right at about 210 yards, which I had been in before. Jay went first and had his usual good drive in the fairway just at the bunker. My drive then went about 220 yards – just over the bunker, and I started to get excited. Jay's second shot landed 30 feet to the left of the pin behind a monster trap. I had a wonderful 2nd shot that landed on the first cut. Jay hit a perfect high-flop shot that landed only 4-5 feet from the pin. I had a lucky nine-iron chip shot that rolled through the snow to about the same distance. I do not remember if we made our putts, but I did not care because we tied the hole, and I was still three holes up with only two holes to play – I had won the match.

The last two holes were anti-climatic. I came out of the zone and realized that I was wet and freezing, that my left-hand glove was soaking, that my expensive new golf shoes were wet inside, and that I had no circulation nor feeling in the toes of my right foot. The wind had stopped, but the light snowfall continued. Jay started shivering – perhaps from both the realization that I had won and the cold. Jay won the last two holes – and we jumped in the car and drove home to his house. By the time we arrived, the temperature outside his house had warmed to 37 degrees.

For the record, Jay shot something like an 88, and I had a 98. Jay is the better golfer. But, thanks to golf's handicap system and the rules of match play, I won the match by one hole. I do not know if I should conclude that snow golf is my element – but that day was one of the best golf days of my life, and I stayed in a happy glow for the rest of the week.

I wonder if snow golf could be a demonstration sport at the next Winter Olympics….

# The Terror Of The First Tee

There is too much pressure on the first tee in a golf match. You only get one swing. It is the hardest shot of the round and with the most challenging club (the driver is the longest club in the golf bag) – but you only get one try. They ought to make mulligans (second shots) legal – at least for the first tee. It would comfort me greatly to know I had at least a second chance on the shot.

Other sports are more forgiving. You get two tries in tennis: You hope to get your first serve in, but if you miss, you have a legal second shot. In baseball, you get three strikes – three swings to hit the ball. In football, a team gets four downs to cover ten yards. In soccer, a team gets five tries to make a tie-breaking goal, and in horseshoes, everything close counts.

It's just not fair. Starting cold, one is expected to step up in front of friends and spectators and perfectly hit the hardest shot in the match – the first tee drive. Golf courses should at least start with short holes so you could tee off with an easier club – say, a 5-iron. Nope – there seems to be a rule that all golf courses start with par 4 holes that require a driver – the hardest club in the bag. One chance, one swing – one opportunity to blow your day or make your match.

For experienced players, it's no big deal – they're used to it, but for inexperienced players, the first tee can be terrifying. You only get one swing to hit the ball: I call it "The Terror of the First Tee."

I learned the first tee terrors when playing golf each summer on Nantucket Island with my older brother. He would bring his family to Nantucket to visit us for a week each summer, and we would play golf every day. We both started golf in our 40s and have played together at different courses for years. The first tee terrors have abated – but there is always tension.

The first year was unforgettable. We were no longer beginners, and we had high hopes. We arrived on a beautiful day mid-morning at the Siaconset (pronounced "Sconset") course. It is a short, nine-hole, 100-year-old public course with stark Shaker simplicity. I love it. Light clouds were in the sky, a 10-mph wind from the Southwest, and a group of 10-15 golfers waiting to tee off. New players would arrive as golfers teed off, and the size of the crowd of people waiting to tee off never seemed to change. The clubhouse was very small – there was only enough room for 2-3 people to pay for their rounds and buy balls or use the restroom, and no place to sit down. The building had a small porch, a grassy waiting area between the clubhouse, and a low wood railing separating the tee-off area.

There were no tee time reservations, but there was a two-foot-long sloped wood rack, and each group would put a golf ball in at the top when they arrived and take it out at the bottom just before they teed off – a simple system for making sure we all played in turn. However, some were suspicious that others might rearrange the order of the balls to tee off earlier, so everyone stayed close to the ball rack and the golfers teeing off only ten feet away. The tee-off area was a little rough – a rectangular-shaped area of hard-pack dirt between two white cubes attached to large spikes stuck in the ground. I don't think they had moved the cubes in the course's 100-year history, and grass had no chance.

The first hole is a 215-yard cow-pasture par 3 – probably a typical hole for a well-played public course. The green is small, but there is ample room for error. The fairway irrigation is 'au natural", and in rainy years, the fairway is lush and green. But in dry years, it is hard-packed like a bowling alley with dry brown grass stubs. Tiger Woods might use a seven iron, but we used our drivers.

When we arrived, I placed a ball at the top of the rack, and we went inside to pay for our rounds. Next, we started the ritual of putting on our golf shoes, selecting balls, tees, and gloves, and taking practice swings.

Siaconset has no practice driving range – not even a putting green. It would have been possible to visit Nantucket's other public course, which has a driving range and practice green – but it seemed too much trouble.

So, there we were – aggressively chopping the tops off dandelions with practice swings while waiting for our ball to make its way down the wood rack to indicate our turn to tee off. We did not talk much, as we were each desperately searching our minds and trying to remember what had worked for us at the practice range at home and what we had learned during our secret lessons.

I was conscious of the noises: Cars were going past on the road, airplanes were landing and taking off at the airport, and seagulls were screeching as they circled in the wind. The waiting golfers kept up a steady buzz of conversation, except when a golfer was about to tee off – at which time the buzz level would abate – for a few seconds. I could hear and feel the steady southwest wind despite no nearby trees.

There were also the sounds of the golfers teeing off. I had a golf coach who said he could almost teach golf if he were blind – by listening to the sound of the club hitting the ball. The best sound is the tight click of a good swing hitting the ball in the club's center. There are others like the cutting sound of a ball being topped, the 'clang" or "cluck" of iron or wood hitting the ball off-center, the digging sound of a club head going through the dirt – or worst of all, the silence of a missed ball – the "whiff."

After a few practice swings, we ran out of dandelions, and there wasn't much to do except watch the other golfers tee off – which, in most cases, wasn't much to see. It was a public course, golf was increasing in popularity, and there were many beginners. Some golfers hit the ball well, but there were many varieties of ugly shots. Those waiting formed an informal amphitheater of spectators – many dreading their eventual moment alone in front of the others – like gladiators waiting their turn to enter the ring and fight the lions alone.

We had mixed feelings as we watched the golfers pick up their balls one-by-one out of the ball rack and then tee off. We had a 15-minute wait, but our ball moved steadily down the rack. On the one hand, we were eager to tee off and start our round, but on the other, we were nervous – in anticipation of the Terror of the First Tee.

Finally, our turn came. I was the host, and to get the suspense over, I rolled my pull cart into the practice area, took out my driver, punched the tee into the hard pack, balanced my ball on top, took a practice swing, lined up, waggled once, started my back swing and swung - and hit the ball about 180 yards in the general direction of the green. Whew, the tension for me was over. Now, the fun began.

My brother purposely strolled over to the hard pack with a concentrated but strained, painful look on his face – his face was pale, and his eyes were hollow. I later learned to remind him to breathe because he would stop due to the tension. Because of everyone watching him, he flushed, and the back of his neck turned red. He put the tee in the ground, put the ball on the tee, and stepped back to take one more practice swing.

He used to have a unique and ugly "lunge" in his swing. I have searched my golf books and websites but never found a lunging recommendation. After one look at his practice lunge-swing, the spectators in the amphitheater became very quiet, and there was a nervous tension in the air.

After his practice swing, he squared off and prepared for his drive. At this point, the tension rose, and I held my breath for fear the noise of my breathing would affect his swing. The other people seemed to sense my tension and became deathly still. The silence seemed to have a life of its own – you could almost feel it.

Maybe it was in my imagination, but the whole world seemed silent. The wind stilled. The seagulls stopped screeching; some seemed to have landed and taken cover. I could no longer hear cars on the road or planes at the airport. I wondered if silent golf wardens stopped them for fear of hurting his swing. Maybe the earth stopped spinning.

Then the lunge-swing started. The tension got to me, and I closed my eyes and tensed my body. But nothing happened. Nothing. No sound at all. I waited, slowly relaxed, started breathing again, and finally opened one eye. My brother was bright red and was bent over, picking up the ball and putting it back on the tee. He had made a massive lunge-swing but missed the ball – worse yet, in front of the non-breathing masses in the amphitheater, the air from the missed swing had knocked the ball off the tee, and the ball had rolled between his legs. The Terror of the First Tee was alive and well in Nantucket.

I did not utter a sound – like mentally severing my vocal cords from my brain. He didn't look at me, but I couldn't watch his second swing, so I turned away. I noticed that most of the other people were now avoiding watching as well. It was like when our parents told us not to look at a welder's torch or eclipse of the sun when we were children because the bright light could hurt our eyeballs. It was just too painful to watch. At least this time, there was a ball contact sound, and I opened my eyes in time to see the second half of a 100-yard dribbler that came to rest in the middle of the fairway.

With no sounds uttered, no apologies offered, and no turning around to look at the eyes on our backs, we grabbed our pull cart handles and were off down the fairway. The tension was over, and we could now enjoy the game.

My brother's Terror of the First Tee never went away, and it increased the next year. Like the emotional build-up and release of an unmarried couple who meet secretly for love one night per year, my relationship with my brother seemed to be defined by the build-up and let-down from the first tee of our summer golf rounds in Nantucket.

The springtime rituals didn't change – more secret lessons and driving range flailing, more long-distance telephone calls that didn't mention the unseen gorilla in the room, the arrival in Nantucket, and the incredible pressure of his first tee shot.

He didn't disappoint me the second year. His tee shot did make ball contact, but just enough of a tick on the inside that the ball, like a right-angle poolroom shot, it rolled ten feet away from him and toward me – I opened my eyes just in time to jump aside to avoid having it roll between my legs.

The third year was even more dramatic. Somehow, the whole crowd knew the drill and was in suspense. Again, I closed my eyes and waited, but this time, I was thrilled to hear ball contact – but on second thought, it didn't sound quite right. For some reason, I was afraid to open my eyes right away. Almost in disbelief, someone in the crowd said, "It's in the air!" Of course, we all half expected next to hear, "It's a bird, it's a plane, it's Superman." Instead, after several seconds, I heard someone say, in a funny tone, "It's on the green."

Stunned and in disbelief, I opened my eyes and looked at the green 215 years away and saw nothing. I whirled around and looked at my brother and the bystanders. He had a funny look on his face, and they all looked 45 degrees to the right at the green for the 4th hole – about 50 yards away at an angle. There was his ball all right – in the middle of the green. Wrong green, of course – but better than last year. As before, we grabbed our golf carts, offered no apologies, and started walking – feeling relieved again that the Terror of the First Tee was over – until next year.

My brother and I still play regularly in Nantucket and at other courses all over the country. We have improved our games and are both 20+ handicappers who love the game but must fight hard to break 100 in any round. I've told him several times that I admire his perseverance under pressure in those early years – for withstanding the Terror of the First Tee.

He's still working on that lunge.

# Blonds on the Golf Course

**An Island golf course**

I received the following letter from my Club's Ethics Committee.

> *"We hope we are not disturbing your family's Thanksgiving holiday, but there is a matter of some concern here at the Club that we have been asked to bring to your attention and request your assistance.*
>
> *You played golf with several guests on Sunday, November 11. We remember it was a particularly beautiful day, and we hope you had a pleasant round.*
>
> *You may not be aware of the excitement on the Island since that day.*

*While the facts are still confusing, it appears that two women, reportedly attractive blonds, "approached" a group of four older male golfers on the golf course. We do not yet know how to define the word "approach," but we do know that the stories and rumors during the next few days reached a fever pitch of older male excitement and fantasizing not previously seen at our Island's golf club.*

*The idea that attractive blond women were "approaching" older males on the golf course seemed to have caused many of our older, perhaps ultra-fantasy-prone, romance-challenged, male members to separate from their senses. The first evening, there were only stories of "mystery blonds" on the golf course. The next day, however, the story had spread. There was an outpouring of men on the golf course – golfers and non-golfers, old and older, alone and in groups, in golf carts and automobiles – all wondering around looking – presumably for the mystery blonds – and apparently all hoping that they too would be "approached" by them – again without any clear notion of what that "approach" would be nor what it might mean.*

*That night, the Island was in a frenzy (of a nature that is totally unheard of around here). Every golf cart on the Island, including a few that had been retired to lawn and errand duty for years, was in use as dozens of older men were driving around in the moonlight looking for the mystery blonds. The older the man, apparently, the greater the separation from reality – like this was their last chance ever for a blond. We've never seen so many octogenarians driving golf carts around looking – looking – looking – for "mystery blonds." The wives were shocked and confused - but also mesmerized.*

*We have had several more reports of sightings – and more "approaches" – to our older male golfers – but we suspect them to be only wishful thinking or geriatric male fantasizing.*

*The Club's Board asked the Ethics Committee to investigate, and we contacted the foursome who were "approached" and asked them what happened. We have quoted their responses – and their reactions - in anonymity below:*

*#1 – 55 yrs old – a non-resident: "I didn't see them at first – but suddenly they were right in front of us – like we were supposed to know them. Then the one driving the golf cart smiled and said, "How-ya doing?" They went off. They just left. They seemed confused, like they thought we would know or were expecting them. I was very upset because they broke my concentration and interrupted our round."*

*#2 – 65 yrs old – a resident: "We were in the middle of our back nine, and suddenly two beautiful, blond-haired women appeared – in a golf cart. The sun was on their faces, their hair was blowing, they were smiling, their eyes were bright and expectant*

*– they were gorgeous. My hearing was bad, and I couldn't hear what they said - but I was the next to tee off after they left. I was completely rattled, and I sliced badly. My partner and I were leading until then, and we lost the round. Now I am upset and wonder if our opponents arranged for them to come at that moment to un-nerve me – which they certainly did. Those blonds cost me some money!"*

*#3 – 75 yrs old – a resident: "It was love at first sight for me. My wife was a beautiful blond in her time. She died last year, and I miss her terribly. They reminded me of her, and just for the briefest instant, I thought she had come back. My heart swelled, my knees trembled, my legs weakened, my throat choked, and tears came to my eyes. There they were, right before us, so beautiful and friendly - my dreams had come true. I wanted to hug them - but I just froze – and then they said something and were gone. I was heartbroken."*

*#4 – 85 yrs old – a former resident: "I've been very ill recently and just got out of the hospital. It was a beautiful day; the sun was shining, the wind was blowing, and there were whitecaps on the Bay. I felt blessed to be alive and have a nice golf outing with my old friends. I saw them coming first, and in my imagination, I thought I was having a vision. They both looked directly at me and smiled. My heart pounded, and for a second, I feared they were angels coming for me – that my time on earth was over – and that they would take me away. But then*

*I relaxed and smiled, and my fear dissolved – what a way to go: On the Island, on the golf course, on a beautiful day, with my friends – and being taken to heaven by two beautiful blond angels in a golf cart – WOW!"*

*I hope you can now understand our dilemma – one consistent story but four different intense reactions - anger, greed, love, and fear - that cover the full spectrum of emotions. This is all we know. The records in the pro shop show that you had two carts and three guests – but there are no records of any other guests that day nor of any women, blonds or otherwise, on the course – either walking or in carts. We have also been told that you had a large bill for the Sunday brunch. Were the two blond women your guests? If yes, did they approach these men? And if so, why?*

*The reason we're writing you is that there is an unconfirmed report that you were seen talking to several women, perhaps blonds, who were in a large dark-colored SUV in the parking lot – and that you were putting two sets of what looked like ladies' golf bags onto a golf cart.*

*Things have quieted down, but the Island may never be the same. We don't know if there were any mystery blonds, if they were on the golf course, if they approached our members, or if the "approach" should even be a matter for the Ethics Committee. We do think, however, that many of our older male members may be permanently changed by this event and may spend the rest of their days secretly looking for, waiting for, hoping for, or more likely, just thinking about or, more specifically, fantasizing about, the mystery blonds - and whether they will return. Frankly, we're just thankful that we did not have any golf cart collisions or heart attacks. If the blonds ever come back, there may be a riot.*

*Whoever the mystery blonds are, they must be something. Truthfully, some women on the Island are jealous – it's been long since anyone paid that much attention to them. Whoever they are – they've sure still "got it"! Their power in igniting the fantasies and passions of our older men was incredible. We would love to meet them...*

*The Board has asked the Ethics Committee to learn what we can and report back to them. You can reach us through the Club Office.*

*We respect your privacy, but if you have any information about this, please call."*

The Ethics Committee

# The Million-To-One Man

We were playing in a golf tournament at a banker's conference. There were 20-25 foursomes of bankers, and it was a difficult course in the Maryland mountains. My business partner Mick had "purchased" some mulligans by making a charitable contribution. We had been playing well recently; we thought we might have a chance of winning because the third player in our group was a very good golfer.

Frank was a last-minute addition to complete our foursome. Frank is slender and of medium stature with glasses and curly hair. He did not look like a golfer – he did not look like a banker either. I had known him for 30 years – initially as an urban planner – and later after he transitioned to commercial lending at a community bank. He had a ready smile and good humor, and I had always liked him.

I didn't know he played golf, and I was surprised to see him in the tournament. I was dismayed when he announced this outing was the first time he had played golf all year. Why had they placed Frank with us? We needed another excellent player in our foursome to have a chance at winning. We were all medium golfers – but erratic. We needed a steady, reliable fourth to be there when we did poorly.

We watched Frank for the first few holes – all his shots were short and went approximately 30 degrees to the right – regardless of which club he was using. We wondered if we could trade him for someone who could help us.

We teed off. The course was hilly, the fairways were long and narrow, and the grass in the rough was long, thick-bladed, and damp. It was a challenging course.

It was a best-ball scramble format, which meant, for instance, that we would all tee off – and then three of us would pick up our balls and all hit the next shot from wherever the best shot landed. The advantage was the game moved faster, and the odds were lower that we'd need to hit out of the sand or rough. However, there was a catch: we had to use each team member's drive at least once on the front nine and again on the back nine.

The three of us seemed to take turns making decent shots and were doing well at the end of the first nine holes. Frank's shots continued to be short and 30 degrees to the right, but one of his drives on a short part four managed to dribble about 100 yards to an area of short rough, so we used that drive. Still, we managed to rescue a par thanks to a good fairway wood shot by the third player in our foursome – whose name I forget.

Frank became depressed. He knew he was doing poorly and hurting our team's chances of winning. We tried to be encouraging, but he knew he was a deadweight just being dragged along – I think that was his phrase.

We came to the 12$^{th}$ hole, a long downhill par 4 with wetlands just in front of and behind the green, so the approach shot was tricky. None of us landed on the green, and our best ball was on the first cut about 20 feet from the pin.

On each green, we did a lot of talking and strategizing about the putt. I often putted first because I had a steady putting stroke, and I would try to establish the line for the others. I'd been lucky twice and sunk 8–10-foot putts, which had helped us. Frank always listened and putted last in turn – like an afterthought. His putts were straighter than his other shots – but it was clear he had not played before that year and that he played only rarely.

On this hole, I went first but misjudged the speed and went five feet beyond the pin – which did not help the others much. Mick putted next, but he didn't do any better. The un-remembered third in our foursome putted and did poorly, so we began worrying about whether we might miss the 2$^{nd}$ putt and end up three-putting.

The three of us walked forward the pin to see which

position to choose for the 2nd putt. We completely forgot about Frank. He said something like, "Wait for me," and then we heard the click of his putt. Something about that "click" sounded a little different – a little better – like maybe he had changed putters – or perhaps my wish had come through, and Frank had been substituted for a real golfer.

I think subconsciously, we all sensed something, and we stopped talking about our next putt and looked at Frank. He was standing on the first cut, holding his putter, 20 feet from the pin, and the ball was moving briskly in the right direction. I sensed instantly that the pace was better than mine – because I had putted so poorly. Frank had a funny look in his eye – like, "Wow, that felt pretty good."

It took an eternity. Like at most resorts, the greens were rough, and the ball bounced a bit – but kept going. We stopped talking and watched the ball – and it kept going. It seemed for an instant that the wind stopped, maybe the birds froze in mid-air, and the earth stopped turning – but the ball kept going. Frank was frozen – could it be? We were speechless – what was happening? And, like the battery bunny rabbit – the ball just kept going. Finally, as if in a groove, it turned a bit to the right – and dropped into the hole.

The earth was in stunned silence. Then, the heavens erupted with cheers. We laughed, shouted, slapped Frank on the back, and danced around. It was incredible. Frank had single-handedly come out of nowhere and saved our hole – maybe our match.

We could not believe it – he could not believe it. He was saying, "I made it," "I made it," "I made it". What he meant was: "I'm on the team," "I'm no longer a dead weight," "I can hold my head high," or like the Memphis janitors in the civil rights protest attended by Dr. Martin Luther King, "I am a Man."

We finally calmed down and continued forward. The next hole was an uphill 350-yard twisty snake with a gully running down on the right side and a hill extending up on the left – with thick bushes and big rocks. It was probably easier to play the 2$^{nd}$ time, but it was mentally daunting the first time. Again, we ended up with our best putt 20 feet from the hole – but at least on the green this time. Again, we went through our procedure of discussing the putt exhaustively. Frank paid more attention this time, but we returned to our previous attitude and ignored him.

The three of us putted again – but again did poorly. Our best shot was four feet away – and uphill. This time, we at least remembered Frank was on the team – so we stepped back - a little more, respectively – and told Frank to go for it. He seemed to be in agony. I sensed that he had not thought about any of his putts before- probably just closed his eyes and hoped – and now he was unsure what to do. He stood there for what seemed an eternity and finally putted.

This putt seemed too slow – but the downslope was deceptive. It was moving slowly – but not slowing down. Could it be? Could he hit two 20-foot putts in a row? The ball was curving ever so slightly – but not slowing down.

Maybe it would end up closer to the hole than our putts – and we would use him to make our par. It kept going, caught the left side of the cup, swirled around, and went in from the back.

Pandemonium broke out. It was incredible. What are the odds of non-golfing, former urban planner/banker Frank hitting two long putts in a row? His putt gave us a birdie, so suddenly, we were looking competitive.

Frank was in shock - or a trance. I do not know if he's ever had any athletic success before in his life – and suddenly, he was the hero of our foursome. He did not say anything – just kept walking with a big smile.

I do not remember the geography of the next hole – only that it was another par 4, and once again, we were all 20 feet from the pin and looking for a birdie putt. We did not say anything this time, but the dynamics were different. Suddenly, we had a secret weapon - like Harrison Ford pulling the gun out of his belt to shoot the swordsman in the Raiders of the Lost Ark movie. We had an advantage. Again, we all putted, and did a little better this time, with one of us ending up only two feet beyond the pin.

This time, without saying anything, we all stepped back, with respect and hope, and looked at the ground, or the sky, or the tops of the trees, or at our shoes, or the hole – anything but at Frank. We did not want to jinx him. Nothing happened; there was total silence. None of us looked at him. Finally, we heard the click of a putt hit properly in the middle of the putter.

This time, there was no mystery, suspense, or doubt. All the cosmic forces in the universe lined up with that putt. It went straight and true – no bumps, no wiggle, no gentle curves – straight as an arrow – and dropped in the hole – like it was destiny – like it was pre-determination, like the golf gods, if there are any, had decided before he hit it that this one was in the hole.

Three twenty-footers in a row – perhaps no one on the face of the earth has done that before – or ever will again. We cheered, we applauded, we congratulated - but it was almost scary or spooky, like we should be looking around to see if there were golf gods in the heavens or perhaps funny little hairy beings with wings and hoofed feet behind the bushes watching us – and helping Frank.

Frank was in a trance – having an out-of-body moment - almost nonchalant – like, "Oh well, I do this all the time." The rest of the round seemed anti-climatic. I remember one hard up-hill drive where Mick used more mulligans than I had remembered that he had purchased to get us a decent drive, but oh well – we had the gods on our side. Frank continued to hit his drives and fairway shots 30 degrees to the right, but he did not have any more miracle putts. Finally, on the 18th tee, I suggested he turn his left hand 20 degrees clockwise on his grip – and his drive went straight – not very far, but straight. He said something like, "Now you tell me," But I have never been confident enough in my own game to advise anyone else.

We ended our round and turned in our scores. I was tired, so I went to my hotel room, took a shower, and had a nap. I was late for the buffet dinner – and was surprised to learn that we had won the tournament – and I had missed the ceremony where they announced the award. I was a little embarrassed about how many mulligans Mick had used – but oh well – the prize was a dozen new golf balls for each of us, and I had lost at least half that many during the day and needed some more.

Frank introduced me to his wife, and I exalted Frank's feats to her, and she beamed with pride. She kept looking at Frank uncertainly and then back at me as if to say: "Are you sure you mean my Frank?"

During the night, the little bit of probability theory that I could remember from statistics classes years ago in grad school started bubbling in my brain. While lying in the dark, I began to compute the mathematical probability of what Frank had done.

The only fact I had was from a short-game golf clinic that Mick and I had taken, where we were told that the probability of a pro making a level 10 ft putt was 50% - or 1 out of 2. I then started to make some assumptions. If the odds for pros making 10-footers was 50%, what was it for 20 handicappers like Mick and me? I figured it was 20% - or one of five. That seemed about right. I might make a ten-foot putt every $5^{th}$ try. What would the odds be for a once-a-year golfer like Frank to hit a 10-footer? Despite Frank's phenomenal accomplishment – I guessed 1 out of 20 – or 5%.

So, what about a 20-footer? Would it be twice as hard as a 10-footer? Wouldn't it be exponentially harder? If it is a 50% probability for a pro to hit a 10-footer, is it a 20% probability for him to hit a 20-footer? Do pros hit one of five twenty-footers on TV? I am not sure. What about 20 handicappers and 20-footers? I guessed a 5% probability, although I am not sure Mick or I sink 5% of our 20-footers. What about Frank? I guessed it is a 1% probability, or one out of a hundred, for a non-golfer to hit a 20 ft put.

My probability assumptions are summarized below:

| Length of Putt<br>Probability of sinking | 10 ft | 20 ft |
| --- | --- | --- |
| Pro player | 50% | 20% |
| 20 handicapper | 20% | 5% |
| Once/yr player | 5% | 1% |

What about hitting three of them in a row? I remembered that the formula is multiplying the probability of the first event times that of the second event to get the answer. For instance, what is the probability of flipping a coin twice and getting heads both times? It is 1 out of 2 or 50% for the first flip times one out of two or 50% for the second flip – for a probability of one out of four or 25%. It can also be stated in percentages as 50% times 50% = 25%.

The formula is:

$$\frac{1}{2} \times \frac{1}{2} \times \frac{1}{2} = \frac{1}{8}$$

What does that mean for Frank? It means that the probability of his sinking the first 20-footer was 1 out of 100 – or 1%, the probability of the second one was 1 out of 100 or 1%, and the probability of the third was also 1 of 100 or 1%.

The formula is:

$$\frac{1}{100} \times \frac{1}{100} \times \frac{1}{100} = \frac{1}{1,000,000}$$

Re-stated: 1 out of 100 x 1 out of 100 x 1 out of 100 = 1 out of 1,000,000 – or one in a million.

In other words, the odds of what Frank did were a million to one – Frank was our million-to-one man!

I have tested this math with people more knowledgeable about statistics and probability theory than me – but have not been challenged – so it must be close.

I have seen Frank at various banking functions since then, and I always say something about his being the million-to-one man - and I re-tell the story for whoever is nearby and will listen - which earns a big smile as he pleasantly remembers his moment in the sun.

It was a day we will never forget, but I still feel guilty about Mick's extra mulligans.

# Ice Golf

I knew I was in trouble.

She just said, "I'll play," in response to her brother's invitation to us to join him for a round of golf at 7:00 am the next day. He wanted to watch his daughter in a rowing competition at 10:00 am, but he had time for nine holes if we started early.

Was it the wine she had at dinner speaking? Did she understand how cold it would be? Would she have a miserable time and be deterred from golf forever? What should I do?

Normally, I would be enthusiastic about an early tee time. Not this time, however, because it was mid-November, we were in Philadelphia, and I had checked the weather forecast and knew the temperature the next morning would be below freezing. I have often said that my cut-off for playing golf is 45 degrees with the sun shining and no wind – but this wasn't going to be even close.

She is a tall, fit, slender, 50ish, attractive redhead with a Ph.D., a quick mind, long legs, a good sense of humor, and a pretty smile. She has a good golf swing and is past being a beginner. She had some good shots the day before, which had obviously stayed in her mind, and she was starting to get "hooked" by the game – which was all right with me – if, hopefully, she also got "hooked" on me – or at least continued to play golf with me. I'm recently single and am exploring this new world.

We were in the living room of her brother's large house in Bryn Mawr, an old affluent Philadelphia suburb, after enjoying dinner at the stately and famous Marion Cricket Club, which, with an imposing grand facade, looks the way an old private club should look.

We've played a half dozen times together before – usually walking at my club near Baltimore – and one weekend in Key West. She's in the market for new clubs, but most times, we split my bag, and she uses the odd clubs, and I use the evens – and we share my driver. Today, it didn't matter because we were riding in the same cart.

The following day, the thermometer outside the kitchen said 28 degrees. I suggested that it must be broken, but her brother's wife, a good-looking, no-nonsense family doctor from England, informed me dismissively and emphatically, in her wonderful English accent, that it was not broken – thank you very much. She has more common sense – and she flatly declined to join us. Her husband, the brother, a shrewd litigator-lawyer and golf enthusiast, had complained about his game the day before and seemed hopeful he could rectify his problems today (hope springs eternal?).

They were raised in New Hampshire and were not deterred by cold weather. Although I am originally from Michigan, I have lived in a more temperate climate (Washington, DC) for a long time and didn't want to play - but she is a new relationship, my manliness was at risk, and I didn't know a face-saving way to stay warm.

It was sunny and clear but very cold when we arrived at his country club at 7:30 am. The course had been very wet the day before, with standing water along the cart paths, soggy fairways near the creek, wet sand in the traps, and very slow greens.

I had two wool sweaters under my insulated windbreaker jacket and a solid hat, and, ironically, considerable confidence because I knew I played well in adverse weather because I was forced to swing slowly because of all my clothing. She had her long underwear from skiing, a sweater, and a windbreaker, but I didn't think the sweater was warm enough. I expected her to start trembling from the cold at any moment.

It was too cold for the practice range because it was on top of a windy hill, so we started cold, literally and figuratively, on the first tee. I swung slowly, hit a decent drive, and started to get into the spirit of playing golf.

However, my mood changed abruptly when the cold wind bit in as we started driving down the cart path in the golf cart, so I drove with my left (golf glove) hand and put my right hand in my pocket to keep it warm.

The reality of the conditions hit me on my second shot – a high 8-iron approach that went left of the green and into the trap. Instead of the dreaded sucking sound of the ball burying in the wet sand from the day before, there was a "whack" sound as the ball hit the hard ice in the bottom of the trap, bounced 15 feet in the air like a cart path bounce, and landed in the longer grass between the traps. It was my first time seeing a golf ball bounce out of a sand trap.

The second surprise came on my third shot when I chipped. Instead of the slow greens from the day before, they were like glare ice, and the ball wouldn't stop. It went scooting past the hole and into the long grass again – on the other side of the green. Frozen greens were a new experience, and it was hard to adapt to putting on a rolling, sloping skating rink.

I like to have a wet towel to clean my clubs – but the clubhouse was closed when we teed off, and there was no drinking water on the course. However, the cart broke the ice in a puddle near the cart path near the first tee, so I used that to wet my towel. Unfortunately, it had already frozen when I tried to use it on the second tee – a clue that the temperature was still below 32 degrees.

After teeing off on the 2nd hole, I tried to diplomatically suggest to the brother that "she" was cold and I didn't think "she" was dressed warmly enough, and that it was OK with me (the gracious and accommodating out-of-town guest) if we hung it up and went home. This was the lowest fairway on the course – in the shade along the creek – and surely the coldest. He looked at me in surprise and dismissed me summarily by saying that "he" wasn't that cold, and "he" was fine. I had no recourse but to choke back a whimper and keep moving. I noticed, however, that my toes were getting cold and that my khaki pants seemed woefully thin against the cold wind. I wished I'd worn my skiing long underwear.

It warmed up a few degrees, and the next two holes were at a higher elevation, so we were in the sun, and my mood improved. She was doing well – even though she initially jogged between holes to stay warm. I persuaded her to sit with me in the golf cart, and I put my arm around her – ostensibly to be affectionate and encouraging – but truthfully to draw heat from her warm body. I

My toes were getting colder, so I started leaving the cart on the cart path on each hole for a toe-warming walk to my ball.

After an hour and a half, or around 9:00 am, the sun was out, the temperature had warmed to at least 35 degrees, my towel had thawed so I could clean our clubs, and it seemed almost balmy. Life was good!

We only had time for nine holes, but as it got warmer, the coldness of the first two holes seemed but a memory. She hit more good shots and seemed happy and oblivious to the cold. I managed to survive without letting my "wimpiness" deter either my enthusiasm for the game or, apparently, her interest in me.

We're playing again next weekend – and I'm hoping it will be much warmer – at least above freezing!

# Snookered Again

The Anglers Club at Ocean Reef on Key Largo, Florida, is an elegant old fishing club. It has Tarpon and other large salt-water game fish on the dark wood-paneled walls in the lobby. There is a beautiful dining room, an outdoor patio, a pool, a croquet court in front where men dressed totally in white clothing wage combat, the boat docks, and the beautiful waters of Card Sound. Ernest Hemmingway had been a member. Off to one side, like an afterthought, is a large 9-hole putting green. The setting on the patio, overlooking the putting green with the waters beyond, is idyllic.

We had visited our friends there for several years. The husband, Tommy, a real estate investment banker, belongs to a long list of prestigious clubs up and down the East Coast. He's a good athlete but is not a golfer. He plays some tennis, but the sport that gets his juices going is sailing the 12-meter sailboats from the America's Cup – the "sport of kings." He is fun and companionable but also smart and cagey. I like discussing global economic investment strategies with him, but I don't have much to invest globally or anywhere else.

After a leisurely lunch on the patio, I studied the practice green. It was oval-shaped, approximately 20 yards across, and 40 yards long – less than half of a football field. There were nine scattered holes with three-foot-high flags in each. The grass was longer than a country club green, and the grass blades were wide – unlike the more familiar bent or Bermuda grass we play on in the North. The surface was flat, with a mild downward slope from the clubhouse towards the water.

I suggested Tommy and I play a game, so we opened the large wood chest that held the equipment, took out some rusted putters and golf balls, and started practicing. Most of the holes were 15-25' putts. The putting surface was slow, but after a few tries, I felt I understood the pace necessary to handle the slow green.

When I play on a new course, I test the green speed by finding a flat area, then hitting the ball with a steady stroke with the club moving from my right to my left foot – with the ball right in the middle. On most greens, the ball goes approximately 20 feet. On slow greens, it's less, and on fast greens, it is more. I then adjust the length of my putting stroke based on each green's distance and speed. If I add an inch of backstroke, it goes approximately 2 feet further.

Tommy is not a golfer; he was only on the green with me because he is the consummate gracious host – and I was the guest. I watched him carefully and decided he had no strategy for judging distance as his balls randomly ended up ten feet short of the hole, 10 feet past, or on either side.

I estimated I could putt well enough to average two strokes per hole. I should be a good enough golfer to get my first shot within 2-3 feet of the hole and sink it with my second shot. I figured Robbie would get a few twos, but mostly threes, and that I might get lucky and sink a long one or two. I play golf often, and although I'm not very good, I decided that a fair match was for me to give him one stroke per hole – and we'd bet one dollar per hole. I figured I would likely lose $2-3, but Tommy was a club member paying for lunch and letting us stay at his house, so that was a small price.

We announced the competition, and although the wives were sitting on the patio overlooking the green, they were engrossed in talk and paying no attention to us.

We started our match, and I first noticed the big change in Tommy. He wore loose-fitting deck shoes and shorts, whereas he was casually hitting the golf balls before. His posture and stance changed dramatically during the match – money and pride were at stake once we kept the score.

He tightened his stance, swung carefully, and started hitting the balls much closer to the cup. On the first hole, he scored a three, and I scored a two – which meant with his one stroke per hole that we tied – which "pushed" the dollar for that hole forward to the next one. On the second hole, the same thing happened, but he nearly scored a two, and I nearly scored a three.

I realized this would be harder than I thought and might need help.

On the third hole, we each got a two – which meant he beat me – and won three dollars because we tied on the first two. I started to worry.

The rest of the round was in a blur. I played well and got twos on most of the holes, but he played well also – and either tied me, which pushed the money forward, or beat me by getting a two. We went double or nothing on the last hole to whittle my debt down – but he beat me again by tying me.

There I was – I had lost 10 dollars – to a non-golfer. I'd paid money at the end of rounds of golf before, but I'm cheap, and the amounts were never more than $2-3. This was the most I ever had to pay out. I was embarrassed and humiliated. Golf is my game – Tommy is a sailor, not a golfer – and I was paying out. I didn't even have $10 and had to borrow it from my wife.

A few months later, I commented that I'd learned something about Tommy that day in my Thanksgiving dinner toast. Although he's usually the genial host, when money is at risk, he becomes a different, highly focused, and competitive person – the real Tommy. I'm not saying that he set me up like a sucker with his poor putting during practice and then closed in for the kill when the betting was on – I may never know.

The next year, I was determined to improve without being outfoxed again. Tommy's nephew Reg was with us. I'd played a few rounds with Reg the days before and knew he was a good golfer – a ten handicap – compared to my 23.

Before the match started, we had a long argument about the rules of engagement and the terms. Poor Reg didn't want to get in the middle of the negotiations, so he waited us out. Tommy had said when we sat down for lunch on the patio again, something that did not seem unusual then, but in retrospect, I wonder. He said: "One guy gets his choice of clubs, and the other gets his choice of balls, OK?" It seemed reasonable to me then – but little did I know.

After our lunch and negotiation of terms, Tommy disarmingly said, "You get your first choice of putters." I thought he was a nice host – which he always was. I still didn't get it. I walked over to the box, selected a putter, and waited for them to select putters. There were only 3 or 4 putters, and none were in good shape.

Then Tommy said, "We get the first choice of balls." He and Kip reached in, picked up golf balls, and walked onto the green.

This is when my trouble started. I reached in and picked up the third and last ball. I realized instantly that something was wrong. It was round and white, but it didn't look right. It was smooth and did not have dimples like a golf ball. It was a little larger than a golf ball, heavier, and made of something else – like wood or marble. It was more like a pool ball, specifically a snooker ball – than a golf ball.

I was in a state of shock. I thought about looking back in the box, but I knew there were no more golf balls because I'd already checked. I thought about asking at the pro shop, then remembered it was an Angler's club – not a golf club. My last thought was to run to my car, open my golf bag in the trunk, grab a Titleist, and run back – then I remembered that Tommy had suggested leaving my clubs in the house – something about needing the trunk room. Was that deliberate?

I took a few practice putting strokes. The ball was round and rolled straight but much heavier than a golf ball. Also, instead of the nice "click" of a putter hitting a golf ball, there was a distinctive "clack."

My heart was pounding. Had I been set up again – for the second year in a row or was it just an unfortunate accident?

The match was abominable. We went "click-click-clack" around the green. Tommy and Reg putted on their golf balls, and I put on my snooker ball. I forgot our complex scoring system and stroke allocation formula in my desperate attempt to adjust my putting game to the snooker ball. And I never did figure out my formula for putting correct distances.

Thankfully, the round ended. I ended up paying cash to both Tommie and Reg. I don't know what the score was. Afterward, my respect for Tommy increased. While it might have been a strange coincidence, I may have witnessed the perfect execution of a carefully organized and implemented long-term plan. It must have taken months of planning to think up the right lines, set me up, organize the putters and balls, and execute the plan.

It is a beautiful club, and Tommy was always a congenial host, but both literally and figuratively – I'd been snookered – again.

# My Almost "Perfect Game"

The phrase "Perfect Game" is from baseball and has a defined meaning. A pitcher has pitched a perfect game if he (or she) has allowed no hits, no runs, no walks, and no errors – so that not one of the opposition team ever got on base. A perfect game is even better than the more widely known "no-hitter," where runners may get on base by walks or errors, but, as implied, there were no hits. Both are very rare – especially perfect games - I'm guessing there are maybe only one or two no-hitters in major league baseball each season – and fewer perfect games. My "almost" perfect game was in golf – so the phrase is a stretch – but it was one of my most exciting golfing rounds ever.

First, some background: I belonged to a small private

club on an Island in Chesapeake Bay between Baltimore and Washington, DC. It only has nine holes, but two sets of tees on each hole at different lengths, so one can play 18 holes and not use the same clubs for each round. It was designed by Charles Blair McDonald, the first US Amateur champion – who later became a famous golf course designer. It has beautiful water views, is short at 6,000 yards, is surprisingly hilly, and they recently added 10-11 new fairway bunkers – as if we need more of a challenge.

I love walking nine holes there – either alone or with friends – particularly an attractive brunette with a pretty smile, who I like a lot, who I've been seeing for over a year, who is a beginner, who plays golf as an accommodation to me, who I rake it out for when she rolls in the sand, who has too much hip waggling in her swing, who gets tired after 6-7 holes, but who hits enough 100+ yard drives to keep her coming back with a smile.

I am a mediocre, but happy and enthusiastic golfer. The euphemism is "high handicapper" – I usually only keep score for the first 4-5 holes, then hit some bad shots and throw away the scorecard. My goal is a bogey round – but I have never done it. I am 64 years old and in decent health, but I am 10 lbs. overweight and was never much of an athlete. The only exercise I will consistently do is to walk nine holes with a pull cart at my club.

Why do I call this an "almost" perfect game? A perfect game at my club would be to hit 7 of 7 fairways on the par 4 and 5 holes, 7 of 7 greens with approach shots, and both greens on the two par 3 holes. In my "almost" perfect game, on one sunny day in July, I came as close as I ever will to a golfing "perfect game."

Fairways: I hit 6 of 7 fairways with good drives. I claim special dispensation for the 7th drive, as explained below.

Greens: I hit 8 of 9 greens (if one counts the first cut).

Part 3s: I hit both greens on the par 3 holes.

Sadly, I putted poorly – with several three-putts. Usually, putting is the only decent part of my game – so I ended up with 45 or nine holes – far from a "perfect game."

My round is summarized below: On the par 4s and 5s, I had good drives – except #7, and on all the part 4s and 5s, I hit the greens – as defined. On both par 3s, I hit the green. To put this into scale, it is like Tiger Woods having birdies on every hole with an eagle on the par 5 hole.

| Hole | 1 | 2 | 3 | 4 | 5 | 6 | 7 | 8 | 9 |
|---|---|---|---|---|---|---|---|---|---|
| Length | 370 | 430 | 170 | 420 | 380 | 160 | 320 | 520 | 400 |
| Par | 4 | 4 | 3 | 4 | 4 | 3 | 4 | 5 | 4 |
| Hit Green? | yes | yes | yes | yes | yes | yes | no | yes | yes |
| Good Drive? | yes | yes | no | yes | yes | no | yes | no | yes |

I had some lessons during the winter at a golf clinic – which uses technology to evaluate and improve one's swing. They put electronic monitors on my wrists, shoulders, and hips, recorded my swing, and then graphed it compared to better golfers. Their goal is to have the hips turn first, then the shoulders, followed by the arms. If you watch Tiger Woods in slow motion, his hips turn first, then his shoulders, and both are past the ball before the club makes contact. It is easier said than done in one's 60s.

We hit balls into a net, and the cameras and computers show us on a monitor what the shot would have done – if it had been on a fairway. Also, they have rooms with TV cameras and computer monitors that record one's swings from the side and back – then replay it in slow motion – so one can see and analyze one's faults.

It had taken me a long time to absorb what I had been taught – much of which is counter-intuitive. For instance, they said I had too much hip turn in my back swing – which I had to reduce – to create tension between my hips and shoulders – and thus more torque in my swing – whatever that means.

Also, I was told to hold the club down in my fingers – not the palm of my hands where I had worn out dozens of golf gloves over the years – it's so hard to change long-established bad habits. The most important change was to slow down my backswing and swing speed to about 70% of what it had been. Also, I played with an eight-handicapper recently and noted that he hung his arms straight down for every swing – which seemed to help me.

What is the most counter-intuitive concept in golf? If you slow down your swing, the ball goes further. Why? I guess because one has higher odds of hitting the center of the club and hitting it straight – instead of the many undesirable alternatives.

What is my swing thought? Some say you should not have one. It is my right knee – creating tension against it in my backswing.

My last "trick" on my almost "perfect game" day was to open the club at the top of my backswing – so that the club face was in the same direction as my body. I do not remember who taught me this or whether it just evolved independently – but it seems to help.

Somehow, on this warm day in July, it all began to come together.

I often get a good drive on the first hole – perhaps because I remember what I have been taught in class and swing slowly – and I usually deteriorate from there – perhaps because I start swinging harder.

The first hole is a cow pasture – with lots of room for slices on the right. On this day, I had my usual first-hole drive, and pleasantly, my iron shot landed in the first cut. Sadly, I then three-putted.

The second hole has a road on the right – and I have probably put a hundred balls across the road in the front yard of the third house with high-slicing drives. Today, I had another nice drive and put my 21-degree fairway wood on the first cut – and three-putted again.

The third hole is a par 3 over a tidal pond, but this time, for the first time in hundreds of rounds, the tee-off markers were back at 170 yards – not the usual 155. I hit a lucky 18-degree fairway wood shot, which is usually suitable for 175 yards, and although it was a line drive, it stayed on the green – and I got a par.

The fourth hole is a par 4 with a deep gully on the left side before the green and a row of pine trees on the right. Usually, my first drive slices high above the pine trees. Again, I had a nice drive, and my beautiful 7-iron approach shot landed on the green – not in the first cut. I two-putted for a par.

The same thing happened on the 5$^{th}$ hole – a long, straight part four with water on the right.

On the 6$^{th}$ hole, a 160-yard par 3, which always seems longer than its official distance, my 6-iron shot landed a foot from the hole – the closest I've ever had to a hole-in-one.

Emotionally, I withdrew - into denial, like I did not want to talk about or even think about the incredible round I was having – because I'd had so many good starts before that ended in disappointment. I was afraid I might jinx it – and would ruin it.

The 7$^{th}$ hole is the make-or-break-it hole – the dreaded "wedding cake." It's a short part four, but one's second shot must demonstrate perfect "target golf" and land on top of a three- or four-story wedding cake –

which is surrounded on the sides and back by a ring of sand traps 10' below the green. I will never forget being in the trap once, with my 20-ish son standing up on the green, looking down at me, and hitting it four times only to see it go part-way up the bank and roll back down to my feet. My son was amused, but I finally picked up my ball and walked to the next tee - another round ruined by the wedding cake.

I've never considered myself a good enough player to play in my club's tournaments. Still, I'd been told that in competition, some players avoid the risk of hitting the top of the wedding cake and play for a bogey by safely punching it halfway up the hill on their second shot – then pitching on the green and two-putting. I will remember that if I ever get up my nerve to play in my club's tournaments.

I had another good drive on the 7th – and was facing the dreaded 2nd shot. However, I was confident that the up-and-down 70-yarder that I had done well on previous rounds and which I had specifically practiced on the practice range was almost a sure thing. Sadly, it was not. I missed on the right and, incredulously, was in the sand trap only a few feet from the dreaded spot where I had given my son such amusement.

Facing the prospect of ruining my best round, I hunkered down in the sand and tried to concentrate. This was very hard-packed sand – with no chance to get under it with a level swing like the soft, fluffy sand at my wonderful Sankaty club in Nantucket. I remembered to descend at a sharp angle – and the miracle of miracles, the ball jumped high enough to clear the edge of the green and roll ten feet past the hole – and I two-putted for a very happy bogey and was feeling good again.

Disaster struck immediately. I was standing on the 8th tee, looking at a long dogleg left part five, and my attractive brunette companion, noting that I'd had some better-than-usual shots, commented on how I was doing remarkably well and then innocently inquired what I was doing differently. She then looked at me with a pleasant smile, expecting an answer. She had been with me on previous rounds and seen how I usually dribble, slice, hook, stumble, and curse around the course.

I tried to stay withdrawn in my emotional box – in my "zone" - in denial – to repel her question with a mental shield – to hold my concentration. Where was the "force" when I needed it? I do not know what I said, but the damage was done. I guess I said something - then I ended my streak of great drives and sliced my drive into the woods. (Don't fathers teach their daughters about not jinxing a pitcher during a no-hitter? Or is that a "guy" thing?)

To make it worse, I walked to where the ball went in the woods, hoping to find it, dropped another one, and promptly hit a second shot into the woods – again a slice from swinging too hard.

I then took a deep breath, re-grouped, hit a tremendous 3-wood shot with a slow swing, hit a beautiful high eight iron onto the green, two-putted – and was back in my game.

The 9th hole is up a ski slope – or so it seems. One's second shot must go higher than the wedding cake's 7th hole – like up a four-story mountain. I had a great drive; I hit the green with my eight iron and two putted for another par.

So, I ended up in euphoria – my version of an almost "perfect game." My best ever – and more importantly, I think I understand why I played better and am hopeful I can repeat it. Hope springs eternal in the mind of the graying golfer.

I am playing with my sons and business partner in a few weeks in Nantucket – if I can, remember to swing more slowly...

# My Favorite Place In The World – The Practice Range

My favorite place in the world, where I would want to be if I only had an hour to live, is the practice range at the Sankaty Head Golf Club in Nantucket, Massachusetts.

Sankaty is a magnificent old course and is included on one list as among the world's top 100 "classic" golf courses. It's on Nantucket Island, an exclusive summer vacation site off Cape Cod, Massachusetts.

The golf course is adjacent to the famous Sankaty Bluff lighthouse in the small village of Siaconset on Nantucket's Eastern shore. The lighthouse, which has protected ships off the treacherous Georgian Banks sandbars for several centuries, was threatened by erosion. Like the Cape Hatteras lighthouse in North Carolina, it was recently moved back to safer ground. It is America's furthest point East, and I was there at dawn on January 1, 2000, to be the first to see the first sunrise of the new century.

Sankaty is a beautiful golf course. It follows the land's natural contours, with myriad shades of green in the summer and, my favorite time, the bountiful colors of fall.

I play my best golf at the Sankaty practice range. Each time I go there, I work through all my clubs, with most of my shots looking pretty good – then go out on the golf course and get butchered by the course, the wind, the gorse (knotty little shrub bush), the rough, sand, fatigue – and, sadly, my lack of golfing skills.

For me, a round at Sankaty is always a humble and brutal experience. The drama always is – will I or won't I break 100? And if it's windy – I won't. My two 20-ish sons now routinely beat me – although I always have high hopes.

It's so frustrating. I always play well on the driving range. At least 80-90% of my shots do what they are supposed to do. Then I play a round on the golf course and get beaten up. Sometimes, I think I should stay on the driving range and forget the golf course. **Why can't I play as well on the golf course as on the practice range?**

I've been a member of Sankaty for about five years. It took twelve years to become a member, including two years to learn the process, find a sponsor and co-sponsor, find six members who would agree to endorse my candidacy, and later, another six people to write letters on my behalf – and ten years to sit on the waiting list. During those ten years, I played a few times each summer with friends, but I would also visit and wander around – and long for the day, I would be a member.

I now have limited playing privileges in July and August, and I must ration my rounds with guests to stay within my quota. I've changed my schedule of visits to the Island to include more time in June and September – when I have more flexibility in playing at Sankaty. I may be able to get a full membership in another five years.

The club has several excellent teaching professionals. A lesson with the head pro is magical. It's like he has an elixir or fairy dust he sprinkles on me. Time and time again, after a 30-minute lesson, he will have diagnosed my problems, explained the solutions, and have me hitting balls perfectly and consistently on the practice range - but then I go out on the golf course, play a round, forget or fail to execute whatever I was doing correctly at the practice range, and fail to break 100 again.

I can do well during the lesson, but **why can't I play as well on the golf course as on the practice range?**

The tee area at the practice range is extensive - 50 yards wide and 40 yards deep. There are tee box areas about three yards apart across the front – in between ropes on the ground that are shifted forward and back to have the members hitting off fresh turf. There are 15 practice areas, and on a busy day, they are all occupied with members warming up to tee off, taking lessons, trying to fix their swings after problems on the golf course, and some like me who have limited memberships and sometimes go just to use the practice range.

The lessons are at the tee area on the left, and there are color-coded signs on each side indicating the distance to the five target greens or flags. There are three greens out at the range – one at 100 yards with a red flag, one at 150 yards with a white flag, one at 175 yards with a blue flag, and there are yellow and orange flags further out at 200 and 250 yards. There's a practice green surrounded by sand traps 100 yards off to the right – which I don't take advantage of often enough.

I can stand there and drop 75% of my pitching wedge shots on the 100-yard green or first cut, but **why can't I play as well on the golf course as on the practice range?**

The weather at Sankaty is magical. My favorite days are when it's slightly humid, in the 80s, with a light haze and mild wind. I like it less so when it's gray and dark, and the wind is howling from the North – or any direction. I'll play golf in just about any temperature – it's just a matter of dressing appropriately.

The practice range faces South, and the prevailing wind is from the Southwest – or the far-right corner of the practice range – just enough to reduce my persistent slice.

Nantucket is famous for its fog – which sometimes

builds up off-shore and drifts onto the Island. The afternoon light often has an eerily luminescent quality from the sun reflecting on the mists rising off the water, creating a sparkly haze in the sky. There are minuscule hints of color from the sun hitting the moisture in the air – like quick reflections of micro rainbows.

The Island was famous for whaling and then went into a deep depression from the mid-1800s when the whale oil industry died out until the early 1900s when artists were attracted to Siaconset due to the quality of the light – like the South of France.

Sometimes, the fog literally rolls in – like massive cotton balls – one can see the trees beyond the driving range disappearing into the fog. Or, for those with more imagination, one can see the hordes of Orks, the ugly enemy soldiers in the movie Lord of the Ring - Return of the King, storming towards us across the tundra.

I can put more than half of my six iron shots onto the 150-yard green or first cut – but miss completely when on the course. **Why can't I play as well on the golf course as on the practice range?**

I've read several golf psychology books – which tell you that your golf success is a mindset – and you can do what you plan to do and work hard to accomplish. I take golf lessons and fitness classes every winter and think positively about being a better golfer – but it never happens.

Why is there a difference between the practice range and the golf course? Why this enigma? There's an existential point about life here – and the difference between aspiration and actuality and the eventuality of the latter. I wish I understood it.

Sports have many examples where one practices for perfection – and maybe or maybe not achieve it. Pitchers practice their fastballs, tennis players practice their serves, and quarterbacks practice their passes. Golfers practice their swing – and hope.

I've asked for help with my practice range vs. golf course problem. A friend suggested I be kind to myself and quit. Another suggested I live with it. One instructor told me never to use the same club twice on the practice range – because one never has the luxury of getting in a groove on the golf course. Instead, I should imagine myself on the golf course using my clubs in the same order: driver, mid-range iron or fairway wood, wedge, etc. Nothing seems to help me.

I can hit balls consistently and nearly perfectly on the Sankaty practice range, **but why can't I play as well on the golf course as on the practice range?**

The most complex club is the driver – and while it's the biggest, it's also the longest, and I've always had trouble with it. The club heads have gotten bigger and bigger in recent years, and although I've tried the newest drivers many times and bought new oversized drivers for both sons, it took me a long time to get comfortable with them.

The sole exception is the Sankaty practice range. I can stand there and consistently hit high, beautiful drives that land well past the 200-yard flag – but short of the 250 marker – which means that on the practice range, I can consistently hit 230 or 240-yard drives – which I'd die for on the golf course. But **why can't I play as well on the golf course as on the practice range?**

Golf isn't a game; it's a quest – like the search for the Holy Grail or the mirage on the highways in the West. One never gets there nor finds it. No one, not even Tiger Woods, is ever completely satisfied with their game. Perhaps that's why I love it – and keep returning for more. There is always hope. Hope springs eternal. The trick is to remember the good shots and keep practicing.

Years later, a friend explained that the secret to golf is that it is 90% mental and 10% mental. He is right.

My favorite place in the world is the Sankaty practice range. I love being there on a warm summer day – with a mild breeze coming in from the right. I can hit dozens of nearly perfect golf shots – drives, fairway woods, irons, wedges - moving up and down my bag of clubs with ease. It is pure pleasure, it is bliss, it is wonderful – but **why can't I play as well on the golf course as on the practice range?**

# Dad's Last Win

It is hard for a 63-year-old man not to be defeated in golf by his 20ish sons, but on Christmas Day 2005 in Key West, Florida, to paraphrase the hero in Lord of the Rings: Return of the King, that defeat was to be "not at this time and not at this place."

I'd been to Key West before because it has the best odds of warm weather in Florida for a short mid-winter break. Our hotel was on the beach just a few blocks from the "Southernmost" point in the country – or so the sign says.

Hurricanes had damaged the golf course. The palm trees were wounded, bushes were gray, construction was in process near the clubhouse, and, as we learned after we paid, some of the greens were in bad shape. We renamed them "browns".

Both sons are very tall – with beautiful golf swings that send their drives soaring beyond mine. Also, both are in their physical primes – with instinctive and youthful hand-eye coordination, making their close-in chip and pitch shots seem effortless.

I'd been preparing hard for the match. During December, I visited my driving range a half dozen times – in the cold, in the rain, and in the dark. Thank goodness for the covers and heaters over the practice area. I really wanted to beat them.

Rob, 27, lives in Boston and commutes to work in New Hampshire – and I knew he'd had no time for driving range visits. Carl, 24, lives and works in Manhattan, and while he has visited the famous Chelsea Piers practice range – I knew that he would arrive in Key West a little rusty. Last summer, on the spur of the moment, I flew up and joined him for a round in the Bronx – hot and slow – but fun. How many fathers get to list the Bronx in their repertoire of golf courses they've played with their sons? The truth is that I have played dozens of courses, including many with my sons, but I'm not very good, and I haven't ever conquered any of them.

To spice up the competition and focus my concentration, I'd sent them an e-mail the previous week suggesting seven $1 bets, including both by holes and score, the front nine, the back nine, and all eighteen holes - plus $1 on the hardest handicap hole. On Christmas Day, to round the maximum potential loss of $10, I added $1 bets on the following three hardest holes. I really, really wanted to beat them – but my fall-back hope was that I would win at least one or two of the ten $1 bets.

Both sons have beautiful and charming girlfriends who are en route to becoming nurses, and Rob added to the drama of the weekend and his own distraction, by deciding it was time to buy an engagement ring and pop the question. He had the ring expressed from New York to my office in DC for me to carry to Florida, forcing me to lie away all night with the ring hidden in a tennis sock in my laundry basket, fearful that someone would break in and steal it or that I would forget it.

The highlight of his weekend was his proposal to Leslie on the pier in front of the hotel late on Saturday night – Christmas Eve. They were both thrilled and on cloud nine. I, too, was thrilled – but for a different and devious reason – that Rob would be distracted during our golf match scheduled for noon on Sunday, Christmas Day.

It sprinkled early Christmas morning, and I was pleased because I had brought my full rainwear regalia and because light rain helps my concentration and might distract or bother my sons. We got up early, had a big breakfast on the hotel veranda overlooking the beach and the ocean, and opened some Christmas gifts – including three dozen golf balls for me – which last only an embarrassingly short time.

We arrived at the golf course around 11:00 am. Leslie had a permanent smile, and her eyes were glazed. She kept looking at the enormous diamond on her left hand and murmuring, "I'm engaged." Rob, too, was in another world of happiness. Even Carl had picked up on some of their glow. This was perfect for me. Carl and I are about even, but Rob usually beats me by ten strokes. If I ever was to beat him again any time in my life – this was it. He had created the perfect distraction. He and Leslie had been on the phone with family and friends starting soon after midnight the night before and seemingly non-stop since then. They went to the midnight Christmas Eve church service but were so excited about being engaged that they left after ten minutes to start calling people.

Leslie's parents were on a cruise in the Caribbean and didn't learn the good news until that morning. Rob had asked her father for permission a few weeks before, so they were bubbling with anticipation and excitement.

Apparently, the employees at the golf course had better things to do on Christmas Day than taking care of golfing visitors, and we had to retrieve our own balls at the practice range (a large net-enclosed area) before we could practice.

Rob and Leslie were in one cart, and Carl and I were in another. Rob said that Leslie might want to wait at the clubhouse, call friends during the first nine holes, and then join us later. Was it unsportsmanlike of me to ask that she join us because I had paid $28 for her "rider fee"? (i.e. because I wanted Rob to be distracted) Was it unethical of me to suggest that she wait until the $3^{rd}$ or $4^{th}$ hole to ask Rob about the two or three issues in their relationship that bothered her? (I don't think there are any, nor that she heard me). I've wondered, but not lost any sleep, about these questions since.

The first hole is a long par 4 dog leg to the right. I went first, and while my drives usually suck, I got it out there a reasonable distance. Carl hit the sand trap on the right, and to my dismay, Rob hit a beautiful long drive in the center of the fairway. I thought, "How could he do that in his distracted mind?" He must have been running on fumes because reality hit home on his second shot: I heard him yell "fore" and saw a group of golfers at a tee area in the next fairway on the left running for cover. I later learned he had hit a line drive over their heads into the mangrove bushes and lost his ball – with a penalty. I got a five on that hole, Carl got a six, and Rob an eight – so the match was on, and I was ahead.

I was happy to hear Rob ask Leigh if she had $10 – the maximum he could lose for the day. She didn't hear him. I'm not sure she heard anything. She was still in a daze with a permanent half smile, the glaze over her eyes, and a crick in her neck from continually turning to her left to admire her magnificent engagement ring.

We then tied the next few holes, and per a rule clarification requested earlier by Carl, a tie resulted in a "push" so that the winner of the hole following the tie was given credit for winning the previously tied holes.

I didn't pay much attention to the scores because I was trying to concentrate and focus on a steady golf swing. I did perk up; however, after the sixth hole, I heard Rob ask Carl, "Do you realize Dad's won every hole?" I'd been lucky and won several holes after the ties, so I was ahead.

I was worried, though, because I have a ridiculous pattern where I start out well for 5-6 holes, then get tired or lazy, swing improperly and have some bad holes, and then, prompted by bad scores, I concentrate and rally toward the end. This happened again in Key West. Rob, who had played on his high school golf team, finally got focused on the 7th hole and finished the front nine par-birdie-par. The birdie was on a blind par 3 over 130 yards of mangrove bushes.

We had sandwiches and drinks at the turn, and after the 11th hole, Leslie begged relief to sit on the clubhouse porch in the sun and call her friends on her cell phone to spread her good news. I didn't resist this time because I was ahead.

I didn't provide fancy cars for my sons when they were young, but I always ensured they had decent golf clubs. I had my steel shaft irons lengthened for Rob and purchased the same irons over the Internet, but with extra length, for Carl. They both got new oversized drivers for their birthdays several years ago. Rob hits 300-yard boomers with his driver. Carl had an initial "honeymoon" with his driver, but now he sometimes hits line-drive screamers and sometimes struggles like the rest of us. He had a two-month break after graduation last spring and used it to work on his golf game.

We had some animal adventures along the way. The tenth tee is the favorite hangout area for some large Cuban ducks – who, like toll keepers, insist on a few sandwich crusts as their price for permission to tee area in silence. They are large with bright red patches on their heads and can be very loud and distracting if unfed. They can appear threatening if they think bread crusts are in one's golf cart.

We saw hundreds of birds, including seagulls, egrets, geese, ducks, turkey vultures that inhabit the adjacent landfill, and funny-looking little guys we called "dodos." We also saw some painted turtles, but the zoological highlight was a four-foot iguana that crossed the fairway ahead of us on the 9$^{th}$ hole. I first thought it was an alligator. Carl made a half-hearted effort to grab him by the tail, and I had visions of rushing him to the hospital with a poisonous slime lizard bite.

Golf is such a wonderful bonder for men. Women share their feelings; men play golf. I love playing golf with my sons, and I've been pleased that they both play with their girlfriends' fathers – a relationship-builder that can last for a lifetime.

Carl is usually slow to warm up – but the iguana seemed to do it for him, and he did well on the back nine and won both by holes and by score – while Rob fell apart, missing the presence of his true love. I recovered from my middle-third slump and improved toward the end. On the 135 yard, over the water, par 3 17$^{th}$ hole, under the watchful gaze of at least 100 birds, my 8-iron shot landed seven feet from the cup, and I managed a birdie 2 – while both sons missed the green and settled for bogie 4s.

We had so many ups and downs that it was difficult to know the verdict. At the end of the match, Carl, a hedge-fund investor, did the math and announced that I'd won seven of the ten bets –music to my ears. Oh, happy day! He reached for his wallet and handed me some bills – which I declined, saying I didn't want his money – only the pleasure of beating them. By this time, Rob had found Leslie on the porch, and the two of them drifted back to cloud-9 for the rest of the weekend.

There are more important things in the world than golf matches, and this weekend, golf was minor compared to the engagement. Also, there are more essential things in father-son relationships than golf. Both sons are terrific young men, professionally and personally, doing very well – and I'm very proud of them. Their lives are in good order, and we have the luxury of worrying about golf.

To quote President Lincoln in the Gettysburg Address: "The world will little note nor long remember" our Christmas 2005 golf match in Key West. But to me, it was exceptional. With an anticipated future of girlfriends, wives, work, and grandchildren, young men will have less time for Dads and golf, so I don't know how many more matches lie in our future. Also, with the continuing march of time and age, this was probably the last time I'd be able to beat them both – so I'll savor the moment.

This was Dad's last win!

# Our First Round At The Quarry

Our first visit was our most dramatic and exhilarating round of golf ever.

**Introduction**

The young man at the pro shop told me The Quarry was "challenging" when we made our tee time reservation for 2:00 pm on August 21, 2023. That was an understatement. We had just played six different Northern Michigan courses in seven days and felt confident, although a little tired. It was the last day of our vacation, and we wanted to try it.

I am a mediocre golfer; my handicap is 20, and I can only drive 175 yards. I aim to play a bogie round (one over par on each hole), but I am rarely successful. My wife Karen, a petite blond, enthusiastic golfer, appears to defy all known laws of physics by swinging slowly and consistently hitting long, beautiful 150-yard drives.

We enjoy playing golf together, and sometimes she beats me. My wife plays the women's tees, and, as Jack Nicklaus advises, I play the senior tees. Sometimes, it is embarrassing to drive the cart past the men's trees. Younger men, whose drives are 100 yards longer than mine, may scoff at the senior tees, but one wonders what tees they will be playing from when they are 80.

**Northern Michigan**

Northern Michigan is a four-season community with golf courses, ski resorts, snowmobile trails, lakes, cultural amenities, restaurants, vineyards, and other attractions.

My father was a professor and had his summers free. He and my mother had a vacation home on a small lake near Petoskey, where we spent summers when I was young. Now, years later, we join long-time friends from high school for a week there each summer.

Bay Harbor is a fabulous community of 1,200 acres along five miles of Lake Michigan shoreline in Petoskey, Michigan. It was built on a former cement factory and rock quarry site.

Bay Harbor has three nine-hole golf courses: The Preserve, The Links, and The Quarry. We played the Quarry and the Preserve for the first time. Next year, we will try The Links.

**1st Hole**

The Quarry's 1st hole did not initially look formidable. It was a short, dogleg right, with 274 yards for me and 225 yards for Karen. I planned to hit a 160-yard drive and then an 8 or 9 iron shot over the rough to the green with a hope for a first-hole par.

It did not work out that way. My drive was short at only 140 yards, and it went left, away from the green and off the fairway into the longer grass. My second shot was also short, and my ball was lost in the deep rough in front of the green. I took a penalty and hit what would be my fourth shot, which was only 94 yards, but it went left into the sand. It was not a groomed sand trap area; rather, it had soft sand like at the beach, and my ball was half imbedded. I knew I could never get it out, so I committed the frustrated golfer's morally challenging remedy of picking up my ball and throwing it on the green. I knew then that this day would be relegated to history as a practice round, and I had no chance at bragging rights.

Karen struggled on the right side of the fairway, and she also lost a ball. We putted, swallowed our pride, took fresh breaths, and headed to the 2nd hole.

**2nd Hole**

The second hole was short, with only 123 yards for me and 109 for Karen. We both were confident at these distances, but there was a very deep ravine to cross, which was imposing. My first shot was short of the green, but I had a lucky pitch shot to within five feet and made the putt for a par, so I felt a little redeemed. Karen, usually automatic with her 5-wood at 100 yards, struggled on the right side, but she had a nice long putt and felt better.

## 3rd Hole

The 3rd hole was visually stunning and intimidating. For the first time, we could see the golf course was in a valley surrounded by the dramatic high stone walls of the former stone quarry. It was not long at 248 yards for me and 149 for Karen, but my tee box was at least five stories above the fairway, and the fairway sloped away to the right toward the rough. There was a large sand area on the left, water on the far right near the green, and a high quarry wall beyond the hole – a beautiful but imposing setting.

I have a little acrophobia and am uneasy on those high, small tee-boxes. I had a decent drive, but it rolled out of sight to the right. I was afraid I had lost it, but I found it five feet from the rough. Karen hit one of her long, awesome drives straight toward the pin.

I stubbed my second shot and had to hit a third to get onto the green. The greens were fast, and I misjudged the speed, went ten feet past the pen, missed my return putt, and ended up with a 6. Karen did better.

## 4th Hole

Neither Karen nor I remember anything about the 4th hole. The tee boxes were elevated, and we both got 6s, but our memories are blank. We may have still been affected by the stunning initial visual impact from the elevated tee boxes and the Quarry walls on the 3rd hole.

## 5th Hole

The 5th hole was a little longer at 357 yards for me and 300 for Karen, and it was also visually stunning and imposing. It was a long cart ride past the back tees to our tees, but it was still stressful. It was another small tee box about five stories above the fairway, which again rattled me. I almost feel that if I swing too hard, I will fall over the cliff. I should have aimed left to shorten my second shot, but I was so intimidated by the height that I aimed to the closest fairway. It is difficult to estimate the distance from those heights. My drive landed in the fairway but was far from the green.

Karen had another good drive and was 50 yards closer to the green than me. I had a decent three-wood fairway shot but was afraid to try to go 130 yards over the water to the green, so I laid up because I felt confident that I was consistent with my 40-yard pitch shots. Karen also laid up, then went just over the green into a narrow trough at the base of a high quarry wall. She had to take a penalty and two-putt for a 6.

My supposed confidence with a 40-yard pitch proved illusory as I put two balls into the water. I hit my third pitch into the green and two-putted, but I had given up keeping an honest score. At this point, I was excited about the course but had already lost three balls.

## 6th Hole

The view from my tiny, elevated tee box on the 6th hole was unbelievable. I could not see where to go. The distances were 275 yards for me and 191 yards for Karen, but there was no visible fairway or green. I hit what looked like a nice drive toward where I thought the fairway must be, but I later realized it was 45 degrees to the right into impenetrable rough—my fourth lost ball. We drove down to Karen's tee box, where I could finally see the fairway and the green. Karen had a nice drive into the small area of the fairway that turned right toward a button-hook green.

I had a terrifically lucky drive from the women's tee that went past her ball further out the narrow part of the fairway. I hit a lay-up second shot to get closer to the green. Karen's next shot went left into the rough, but I pitched onto the green. I then repeated my stupid trick of putting too far and missing my come-back putt for a 6. I sometimes feel that if the number 6 (double bogey) did not exist, I would not be able to play golf.

## 7th Hole

It was another long cart ride past the back tees to my tee box. Again, I felt embarrassed to be playing from the senior tees. It was a blind dogleg left over a deep canyon, trees, and high bushes. The distance was 295 yards for me and 217 yards for Karen, but her tee box was on the other side of the canyon. Again, I had a nice drive – but in the wrong direction – too far right—my fifth lost ball. The hole sloped downhill, and Karen had a good drive and did well. I do not remember the rest of my shots.

## 8th Hole

The 8th hole is Bay Harbor's picturesque signature hole. They show beautiful pictures of the hole with Lake Michigan in the background. It is short, with only 117 yards for me and 82 for Karen. The hole would be formidable on windy afternoons with the prevailing winds from the West over the lake, but it was not windy when we played. I am usually consistent at 110 yards with a nine iron, and I envisioned a beautiful high-floating shot landing on the green and rolling toward the hole.

Instead, I topped the ball and hit a line drive that smacked hard into the front side of the bank in front of the green – but then rolled slowly to within five feet of the hole. I made the putt and had a birdie. It was ugly, but it counts the same as the pretty ones. I was thrilled – a birdie on the signature hole! I knew that I could not do that again in 100 rounds. Karen struggled and ended up with a long putt across the green.

## 9th Hole

The 9th hole was downhill with Lake Michigan on the left. It was 282 yards for me and 250 for Karen. We both had decent drives, and I had 110 yards for my 2nd shot. I hit a high wedge floater that drifted to the grass on the right of the green, and I could pitch onto the green and two-putt for a bogey 5. Karen did the same.

## Conclusion

So, what is the conclusion? Both Karen and I were enthusiastic and exhilarated about the most dramatic and exciting round of golf in our lives. I had five lost balls, but two were from stupid pitching errors, and two were from not knowing the course. Karen only lost four balls.

Also, I had committed the unforgivable golf sin of throwing my ball onto the green from the sand. I may not be the only guy in the world who has done that, and I was not proud.

We consider this round our "Wednesday" round (In professional golf, the players have a practice round on Wednesday that does not count toward their final score).

The course would be unplayable for me if I could not play from the senior tees – but that is the beauty of golf, as the courses are planned so players of different skill levels can play competitively.

I cannot imagine what that course would have been like a few days earlier in the week when we had high winds coming from Lake Michigan – especially for players from the back tees.

To conclude, we were thrilled and eagerly look forward to visiting again next summer.

# Best 80th Birthday Present Ever

My two golfing friends gave me the best 80th birthday present ever – even though they didn't want to!

I'm the oldest – a few weeks from my 80th birthday, and they are "younger" at 78 and 79, respectively. We are friends from high school and have played twice annually for years – in the Spring and Fall. We've been friends for 70 years!

Jim, a former Michigan State University basketball player, Navy frogman, and Naval officer, lives in Virginia Beach. Bob, a former high school wrestler and software engineer, lives in suburban Washington, DC. We play in Richmond, VA, which is halfway between us. Both are retired – but I'm still working.

I play golf, mostly with my wife, but I'm not very good. I have friends with single or low double-digit handicaps, but I'm not in their league. I did get my handicap down to 19.8 at the end of the summer – but not for long, as it rose quickly back to over 20. I did take a picture of my 19.8 handicap on the computer screen during its short lifespan.

Due to its convenient location, we play at The Crossings, which has a nice layout but is underfunded, with dirt and weeds in place of sand in many traps and poorly maintained greens. They have a plan on the wall for steady improvements, and this year, several of the traps had new sand, as I was to learn later ruefully. The golf course is near a monument marking where Confederate War Cavalry Leader J.E.B. Stuart was killed.

In previous years, we played at Military bases with nice, long open fairways, but security got complicated, so we shifted to The Crossing. Jim's historically been the better golfer, but he hurt his shoulder last winter, so I beat him during our Spring match. Bob is inconsistent – lots of good shots but lots of others as well.

It was upsetting to learn, when we arrived and signed in, that the practice range was closed due to excessive rain, and we had to start without our customary warm-up drills. It was disconcerting for me as I needed 10-15 minutes before playing to get in gear for a round of golf.

The first hole started poorly as my drive skewed to the right, my fairway shot dribbled, my first pitch went over the green and my returning chip shot was short.

Somehow, I managed to sink a 10 ft putt, which saved me. Bob and Jim had their own problems, and we all had bogey 5s.

The second hole was a long par 5, and Jim and I first noticed that Bob was playing very well. He got a bogey 6, and Jim and I got double-bogey 7s – so for the first time in ten years of our golf, Bob was leading. Bob picked up another stroke on us on the 3rd hole with a par – while Jim and I had bogeys. On the 4th hole, we all got bogey but mine was very lucky and required a 25" curving putt.

On the 5-8th holes, Bob was on a hot streak going par-bogey-par while Jim and I struggled. However, his honeymoon ended on the 9th, when he hit two consecutive shots into the trees on the left, resulting in an 8, while Jim and I got 6s, but Bob still ended up four strokes ahead of both of us – 45-49-49 at the turn. I'd had a dreaded "snowman" 8 on the 7th hole, a long par 5 with a buttonhook turn to the left to the green. I hit two good shots, but my third shot was a mis-hit lay-up, and my fourth, which was supposed to be a 70-yard lay-up, went 85 yards into the trap – and it took me four shots to get out and into the hole.

On the 9th hole, we thought Bob's ball had gone left into a 4" deep trench with a creek at the bottom. I handed Jim my extended golf ball retriever, saying I'll let a professional get it – referring to his Naval frog man bomb-clearance work in the Suez Canal. He smiled and scooped up several balls – before I found Bob's ball in the trees.

Jim's shoulder was bothering him, and he didn't really recover, but I managed to start chipping away at Bob's lead. On the 11th, I got six, but Bob got a 7. On the 12th, I had four, while Bob had 5, and on the 13th hole, I had six, but Bob had 8. It was thrilling but suspenseful to catch up. At that point, I knew we were tied.

When we played last spring, I had come from behind during the back 9 to beat both Jim and Bob, and I began to have some hope that history would repeat. I earned another stroke on the 15th and knew I was one stroke ahead. Jim continued to have an off day and wasn't in the running to win.

On the 17th, a par 3 over water, I changed from a six iron to a seven iron for the 135-yard shot. It was 5" short and nearly buried in wet, heavy sand on the upslope side of the green. I was upset because I feared losing the match due to my last-minute bad decision.

Despite lessons and lots of practice, I've never been good at getting out of sand traps. Remembering how they do it on TV, I swung hard under the ball, threw wet sand into the air that landed in my hair, and fortunately, the ball dribbled onto the green. Bob and I tied with double bogey 5s, and Jim reminded us who is usually the best golfer with a par 3.

None of us played well on the 18th, and we all got 7s – but I was still one stroke ahead – I had won!

After I won in the spring, I purchased a $10 golf trophy on Amazon with the inscription "Okemos Seniors - Class of 1961 - Golf Tournament – 1st Place". It's been on my mantle next to a similar self-selected trophy my wife won at a club tournament. I showed it to Bob and Jim before we started, but they weren't very interested. I had assumed Jim would win it and keep it probably forever.

It is embarrassing how good winning that golf match made me feel. I was never much of an athlete like Jim and Bob – and I never earned a letter jacket in high school.

Afterward, I felt guilty that I hadn't commented on and been more appreciative of our long-time friendship and our good health – which permitted us to have our round of golf. I was just too thrilled with my win.

Winning the golf match and keeping the trophy was my best 80th birthday present ever.

www.ingramcontent.com/pod-product-compliance
Lightning Source LLC
Chambersburg PA
CBHW070320120526
44590CB00017B/2760